POWERFUL DUO

AIRCRAFT AND
AIRCRAFT CARRIERS

Plane Book for Children

Children's Transportation Books

BABY PROFESSOR
EDUCATION KIDS

Speedy Publishing LLC
40 E. Main St. #1156
Newark, DE 19711
www.speedypublishing.com
Copyright 2017

The biggest warships in the ocean are aircraft carriers. Let's find out what they do, and why they are needed.

GETTING PLANES TO
WHERE YOU NEED THEM

Airplanes are powerful weapons in modern war. They can arrive suddenly and deliver a devastating attack on an enemy position, or drop bombs on a power plant or some other essential target, and then move out of range of a counter-attack. But what if you don't have secure air bases near enough to the targets you want to hit? That's where aircraft carriers can make a big difference.

AIRCRAFT

As long as an aircraft carrier stays in international waters (a few miles off the coast), it is considered to be part of the territory of the country that sent it. There's no need to get permission to use some other country's runways: planes can take off on their missions just as if they were flying from a base at home. Aircraft carriers can bring decisive force to a conflict in a part of the world that would otherwise be out of range.

EARLY EXPERIMENTS

In the nineteenth century some navies launched tethered observation balloons from ships. The observer in the basket under the balloon would have a much better view for miles around than even from the top of the ship's highest mast. However, the observer was attached to the ship: he could not travel to see what was on the other side of a hill.

OBSERVATION BALLOONS

The idea of an aircraft carrier began to be explored almost as soon as the Wright brothers flew their first heavier-than-air plane in 1903. By 1913 the navies of Germany, Great Britain, and the United States had all experimented with adding short launching strips to existing warships.

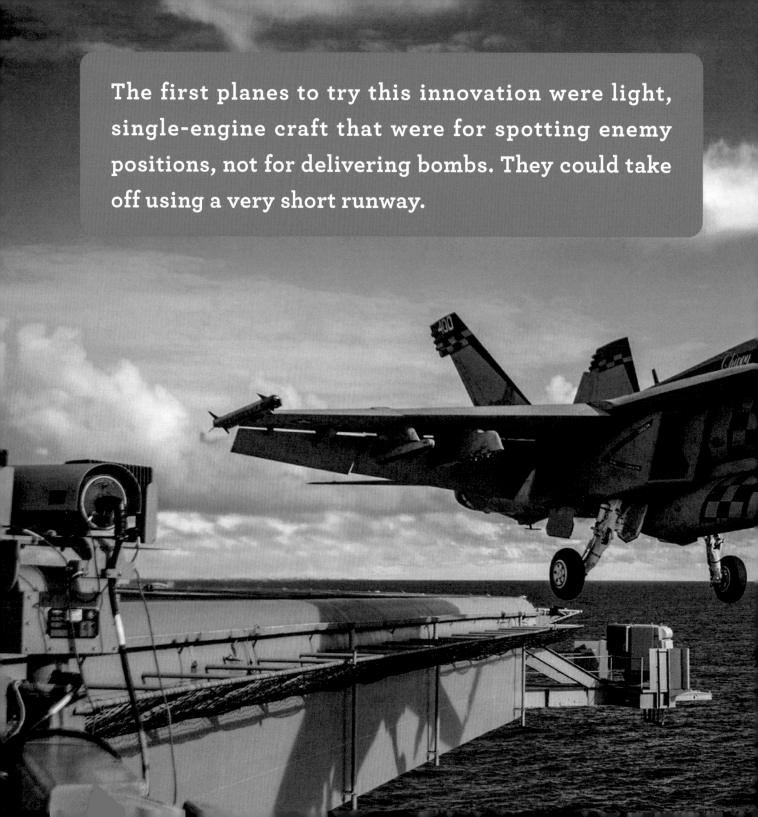

The first planes to try this innovation were light, single-engine craft that were for spotting enemy positions, not for delivering bombs. They could take off using a very short runway.

CURTISS PUSHER REPLICA AIRCRAFT

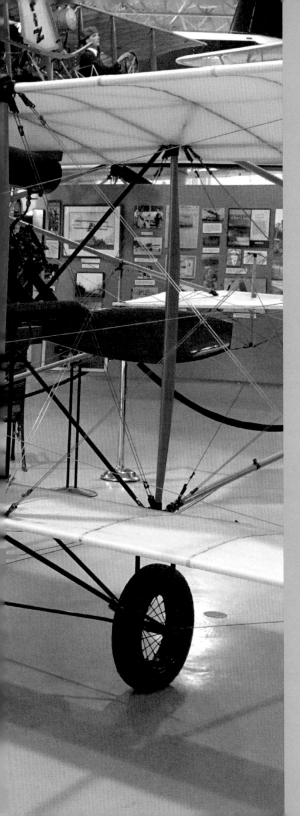

Eugene Ely of the United States was the first pilot to fly a plane off a stationary ship, in 1910. He flew for five minutes and then landed on a runway on land. He was also the first to land on a ship, again stationary, in 1911.

Ely was the first to use the landing system where the plane drags a hook as it runs down the very short runway. The hook (with luck!) catches a cable stretched across the runway and brings the plane to a sudden stop. Ely was able to turn the plane around and take off again, demonstrating the practical use of the landing system. In 1912, Charles Rumney Samson of Great Britain was the first to fly a plane off a moving warship.

EUGENE ELY CURTISS PUSHER

HMS ARK ROYAL

The first true aircraft carrier, rather than a warship with a runway added, was the HMS Ark Royal. The ship launched in September, 1914, and saw action all through World War I. Planes that took off from Ark Royal either landed at air bases or were designed so they could land in the sea near the carrier and then be retrieved.

In August, 1917, Commander Dunning of the Royal Navy was the first pilot to land an aircraft on a moving ship, the HMS Furious. When he tried make another landing, five days later, he crashed the plane and died.

HMS ARK ROYAL

During World War I, the British carried out the first air attack launched from a carrier. Seven planes, each with two fifty-pound bombs, successfully attacked an air base in Germany. Most of the planes then flew on to land at bases in allied or neutral territory, while a couple made forced landings at sea.

GETTING BETTER CARRIERS

Until the 1920s, aircraft carriers were usually created by adapting existing ships, either cruisers or large transport ships. The carrier would have its runway attached above the forward gun positions of the ship, so the carrier was designed to deliver attacks using both its planes and its guns.

By 1924, the United States, Japan, and Great Britain were all at work building ships that were designed from the hull up as aircraft carriers. The ships had substantial flight decks for launching and retrieving planes, a command "island" beside the deck with a control tower from which the crew could guide the ship and monitor plane activity, and lower decks for storing, preparing, and repairing the planes.

HMS Hermes, built by Great Britain in 1924, was the first carrier with a "hurricane bow": instead of having a gun battery below the front of the flight deck, that area was closed in to better protect the lower decks from weather and rough seas.

AIRCRAFT CARRIERS IN WORLD WAR II

Aircraft carriers were not a major factor in World War I, from 1914 to 1918. However, they were a significant element in World War II, from 1939 to 1945. In the European theater of war, carriers escorted convoys from Canada and the United States, helped hunt down German battleships and submarines, and took part in some air attacks on Germany and Italy.

In the Pacific theater of war, aircraft carriers made it possible for Japan to attack targets like the Pearl Harbor naval base in Hawaii, and for the United States to attack Tokyo in response. Read about a key fight involving seven aircraft carriers in the Baby Professor book The 4-Day Battle of Midway; and learn about who was fighting, and where, in The Theaters of World War II: Europe and the Pacific.

PEARL HARBOR

DEVELOPING THE PLANES

Aircraft carriers themselves are not very useful weapons. The ships are far too expensive to send into a direct shooting battle with other ships, or with shore batteries. But the planes a country can launch into battle from carriers can deliver a victory for that country.

To be able to use an aircraft carrier as its base, planes have to have special characteristics. They have to be able to take off from a short runway and to be sturdy so they don't fall apart under the extreme stresses of launching and landing. Most carrier-based planes can fold up their wings when they aren't in use so the carrier can store more of them in a confined space.

Before World War I, most carrier-based aircraft were so light that they could take off under their own power. Usually the carrier turned so it was traveling into the wind while planes launched, helping planes get airborne in a short distance.

Many planes were designed to land in the ocean beside the carrier, which would then try to recover the plane with a winch, rather than trying to land on the tilting, slippery deck.

With increasing demands on the planes to carry more fuel and bigger engines so they could stay in the air longer, and deploy heavier weapons and bigger bomb payloads, unassisted takeoffs became less and less possible. Navies started developing carriers that could help the planes get into the air, and help them land more easily and safely.

Aircraft carriers now usually carry one or more of three types of planes:

CATOBAR

Catapult-Assisted Take-off But Arrested Recovery. The carrier uses a huge catapult to project these planes along the runway deck, giving them the speed they need to take off. For landing, the plane extends a hook which engages with a cable stretched across the deck and stops the plane in a very short distance.

STOVL

Short Take-off and Vertical Landing. These planes usually take off down a tilted runway, like a ski jump, giving them the speed they need over a short distance. The planes are designed to land vertically in a small area, like a helicopter, rather than needing a runway to land on.

STOBAR

Short Take-off But Arrested Recovery. Planes of this type combine the ski-jump launch and the cable-assisted landing methods of the first two types of planes.

AIRCRAFT CARRIERS NOW

Modern aircraft carriers have as many people on them as a small town—and are as big as a small town, too! The largest aircraft carriers, the U.S. "Nimitz" class, are the largest combat ships ever built. They are over three football fields long and almost half a football field wide.

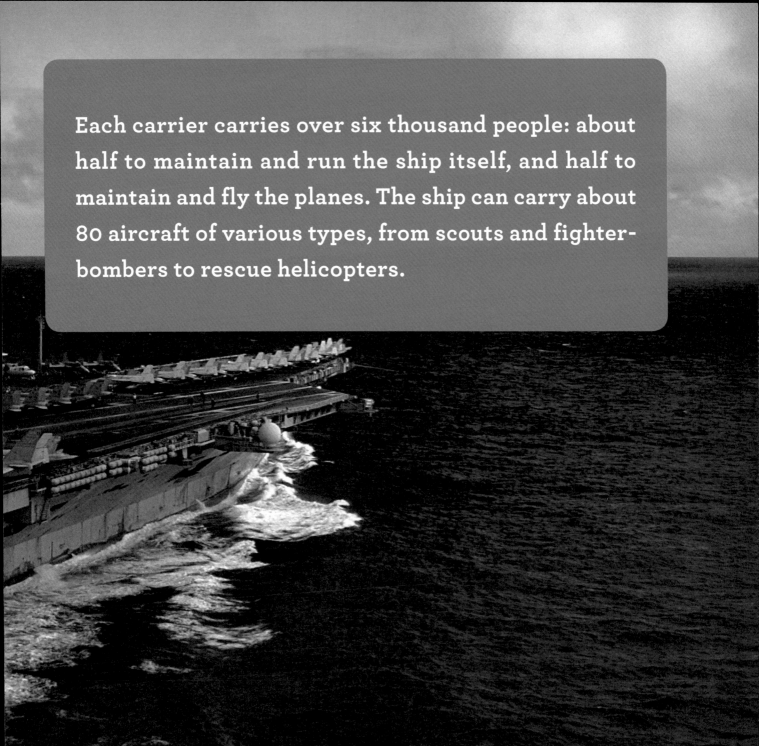

Each carrier carries over six thousand people: about half to maintain and run the ship itself, and half to maintain and fly the planes. The ship can carry about 80 aircraft of various types, from scouts and fighter-bombers to rescue helicopters.

There are about 19 aircraft carriers active in the world's navies at the moment. The United States Navy operates ten of them, with far more capacity than the other nine can provide. There are six new carriers under construction around the world. In addition, many naval ships carry and deploy attack helicopters which can aid in a combat mission without needing a runway for takeoff and landing.

WAR AND TECHNOLOGY

We develop and invent things to meet a need. When people are hungry, we develop better ways to get food. When the weather is often bad, we develop better clothing and houses.

In times of war, the need to develop is urgent. Inventions pop up in all sorts of fields, not just in making better guns. Read about this process in the Baby Professor book: World War II Brought Advances in Technology.

Visit

BABY PROFESSOR
EDUCATION KIDS

www.BabyProfessorBooks.com

to download Free Baby Professor eBooks
and view our catalog of new and exciting
Children's Books